MW01242935

INTRODUCTION

If you've ever uttered the phrase, "I've got to go, and I mean right now," in complete demonstrable sounds of desperation, the following descriptors, and potential chaos may apply to you. Many of you will certainly appreciate the journey described below. This may be a way of life for many, just another day at the office, but for some, it's an occasional occurrence that you've dabbled in over time.

What I am about to describe is simply this…..the end result of a journey that involves what all humans do almost every day. This can best be described as "dropping a load, busting a grumpy, unloosing the caboose, baking a loaf, dropping the kids off at the pool, taking a doo-doo, cut a cigar, build a log cabin, baptize a Baby Ruth, clear the pipes, drop a deuce, pinch a loaf, take the Browns to the Superbowl, blow mud, build a dookie castle, doo the doo, grow a tail, launch a torpedo, prairie dogging" (1) or the most universal saying, go number 2.

The following is a testament to the many who have experienced the exhausting stages and calculated maneuvers that may involve running, waddling, shuffling, briskly walking, turtle walking, peg legging, penguin shuffling, standing still for brief periods, praying, mumbling, fast driving and, many other forms of moving. Your body moves ever so delicately in an attempt to avoid one unfortunate circumstance.

The stages involve calculated moves and are described as a "Defcon." Defcons are stages that a person may experience on their journey to a place where relief occurs. This place can best be described as the "can, office, commode, crapper, head, dunny, loo, jacks, john, latrine, bog, netty, comfort room, restroom, bathroom, khazi, pisser, pot, throne, or the most general term used, the toilet." (2) Your journey is consumed within 6 levels of Defcons and each one has specific physical and mental traits described within.

Throughout these unforgettable journeys, the main objective is to avoid the 5th and final Defcon. Here are words to describe the one unfortunate circumstance you are trying to avoid: "dropping your donuts, sharted, south pole, grumpy poo poo pants, Texas epiphany, riding dirty, Mr. Belvedered, the Susie, fudge stain, buddy dump, temporary latrine, soiled, touched the cloth, brown bomber, fumble" (3) or the most general term or phrase, pooped my pants.

Your journey to avoiding Defcon 5 will most likely transcend your mind and physical body through a rollercoaster of trauma in the hopes that such a stage remains at a far distance. If Defcon 5 should reach its pinnacle and that happens to someone in your presence, you can definitely hear echoes of laughter. This can and will be heard far and away by many. Any episode of that magnitude can certainly be recounted time and time again at the same volume of laughter.

There are 6 Defcons described in Segment 1. There are many combinations within the Defcon stages that you will come face to face with and experience on your journey.

Of course, one wrong physical move, the wrong body posture, the un-flexing of certain muscles, the simple task of bending over, a cough or a sneeze, a slight hesitation, and even a simple traffic light can either make or break your destiny. Many of us know that escaping one unfortunate circumstance requires some strategic planning and maneuvering.

Before you know where you're going, you must first understand exactly where you are, your current situation, and above all, know your limitations. Many people bob and weave their way through the day and much of that time is spent trying to get relief while battling the dreaded Irritable Bowel Syndrome (IBS). According to *aboutibs.org,* "IBS affects people of all ages, even children. Worldwide it's estimated that 10-15% of the population has IBS. Most persons with IBS are under the age of

50. But many older adults suffer as well. The exact cause of IBS is not known. Symptoms may result from a disturbance in the way the gut, brain, and nervous system interact." (4)

Generally speaking, a high percentage of treks to the restroom can be exhausting and tiring. In Segment 1, I will describe the physical and mental traits of each Defcon you may experience as you progress through your journey.

Your goal is to avoid Defcon 5 at all costs. When you're knocking on that door, everything you do, everything you say, no matter what designated restroom stall you enter, and no matter where you park, at the end of the day, all that matters is your ability to relieve yourself without further stress. You'll find that no matter where you relieve yourself, *EVERYTHING* is fair game.

SEGMENT 1
QUANTIFY THE STAGE

This particular journey is filled with unpredictable challenges, good and bad foresight, a basic fundamental of knowing your body, the lay of the land, and your limitations. Just like anything else in life, the experience can be critical.

For those who are well versed in this arena, I refer to you as a *Defcon artist*, a true veteran of the stages. As an artist, you can maximize longevity, manage and create situations that inevitably will defend against the dreaded unfortunate circumstance of Defcon 5. Living in the Defcon world is much different from a novice who enters on occasion. Novices are those who may scramble and have minor battles with attaining relief and their time spent in the Defcon world is limited. This may be the type of person who can go on vacation or a long weekend trip and wait to go #2 until they arrive home. They may also only utilize bathrooms or restrooms familiar to them.

Defcon artists view things a bit differently than many others. For example, the cleanliness of a relief area is generally a non-factor unless extreme and even then we generally won't shy away. When Defcon 4 hits like a category 5 hurricane, we are not considering anything related to cleanliness. This doesn't play a factor and your usage of the area is going to happen, trust me, it's going to happen. The only thing that matters at this point is relief and not the kind that ends in your pants.

When a Defcon artist is in the midst of their journey they look at everything like it has potential for usage. There are few areas that one wouldn't pass up. For example, behind dumpsters, in the woods, any building that has a restroom, basically anything that has cover and concealment. Many times a novice will pass up opportunities based on lack of cleanliness or location and that's where the breakdown or failure occurs and the meeting with Defcon 5 becomes reality.

As a general rule, throughout your journey, one thing to always take notice of is your sense of internal heat. The heat is coupled with the tag-along pressure in the lower region. As you move through or in and out of Defcons you will notice a combination of 4 things that will come into play that you have to manage. Many times they will be simultaneous. They include internal heat, pressure, contractions (shards of pain) and muscle flexing.

Let's take a look at the 6 Defcons that will define and take part in your journey.

DEFCON 1   aka "heads up" stage

This is a rather mild stage for many, but for a true Defcon artist, you know this feeling like no other and all too well as the preparation begins. You still have hopes that it will subside. This is the beginning of a road traveled that can and will change as the environment changes. This stage is generally prompted by what many commonly refer to as a reliable "trigger." Triggers vary from person to person but many are universal. They may include certain foods coupled with stress, physical activity, and possibly involving nicotine or caffeine. As a general rule, this will begin shortly after a meal or a drink.

Physically during this stage, you will experience a very light rumbling in the lower region. The physical experience is very mild and can go undetected for some time. A small percentage may be false alarms but do not downplay what can be the start of a valid Defcon 1. Passing gas, coughing or sneezing is acceptable at this stage and can be done with low to minimal risk.

Mentally you begin to consider if this upset stomach has potential or a false alarm. You cautiously go about your business but take note of your surroundings. You know from experience (just in case this is not a false alarm) you must prepare for your next move. Taking this into consideration, you are careful and somewhat apprehensive to leave the haven of having a toilet at your immediate disposal, if one should be available. This may generally occur at a restaurant or your home. You are now prepared for your move into Defcon 2. This is strictly a "heads up" stage, not much is happening physically or mentally. If you were fishing it may resemble your minnow bait having the ability to move the float, not very alarming.

DEFCON 2 "awareness"

Physically, the rumbling ever so slightly increases and you experience mild sharp pains in the lower region. The pains could readily be identified or described as "contractions." The contractions may be at timely intervals or could certainly be triggered by various physical movements. As the contractions increase, so too will the flexing of muscles in the lower region. Do not be lured into a false sense of security simply because your contractions aren't that severe. Defcon 2 is a true kick start to your journey. It confirms and validates that Defcon 1 was legitimate.

You may have to pass gas at some point during this Defcon but you should always proceed cautiously and consider doing it early in this stage. The notion of doing so is possible but may quickly fade and will soon be off-limits as you reach closer to Defcon 3. This is solely based on your past experiences of complete failure. The internal heat is kicked up a notch.

You may or may not feel a bead of sweat just above the brow.You can feel the pressure building but it's not very convincing at this point, it's present but not screaming. Welcome to the true start of your journey.

Mentally, you know this is a true Defcon and begin self-awareness of your surroundings. You are hypervigilant because you know that you could easily go from a Defcon 2 to a Defcon 4 in a matter of seconds. The questions begin to arise, how soon can I leave? Can I leave before time is up and I must stay? In your head you calculate the time away from home. Where are you going next? Who is with you? Who is driving? What's the toilet availability?

Any joyous laughter occurring at the dinner table is still ok but it is diminishing rapidly. Soon it will be reduced and may completely subside and be replaced by some type of strategic internal calculation. Passing gas is still acceptable but please be cautious with the force used to push/release; this could backfire with relative ease. Personally I wouldn't pass gas if you've been in Defcon 2 for an extended period of time. I would also be cautious about sneezing or coughing, both have hidden force that is uncontrollable.

DEFCON 3 "fish or cut bait"

Physically, it's time to make a definite move. Your facial expressions and body take on a very serious posture. The pressure down below begins an even harsher contraction-like feel which is embodied in sharp pains and becoming more and more frequent between stints. It is becoming rather difficult to move at a rapid pace and in doing so may inadvertently open the cheek area that is so closely shielded by the buttock muscles. Such muscles are working diligently and overtime to stay in place so nothing can escape. Your internal heat is really getting cranked up.

Passing gas, sneezing or coughing is not advisable during any part of this Defcon. If you can pull this off it's based on experience or you're extremely fortunate. Once again, be cautious with the force used because if it's going to backfire this will be the Defcon it will most likely happen simply due to the attempt. You're in the high-risk zone when making any attempt to release anything in the lower region.

If you push the envelope in a high-risk zone and make any attempt to release while not in the act of relief, you could experience what's known as a "*squeesher*" (skwee-sher). You won't find this quoted or referenced in any book or article. I created the word and its definition.

A *squeesher* begins with the intent of passing gas but unfortunately, the release of a small amount of deposit occurs which is immediately self-contained within the cheek area. It doesn't pass the outer cheek threshold and the cloth is not touched or affected. There is no doubt you know this occurred and a slight patting of the rear cloth confirms you're safe, and containment is intact. At this stage of the game, the *squeesher* will remain intact until such time your relief can occur. A "shart" actually touches cloth. This action alone requires immediate strategic calculations. It has become a critical make or break Defcon.

If you're in a vehicle as a passenger, you are quick to point out to the driver that time is of the essence. As the driver looks over he/she may see what appears to be a surfboard. Your mid-section is raised from the seat in an attempt to maintain a solid flex in the buttock area. The alternative is to puch your buttocks so hard against the seat and you're slouched down to maintain constant pressure. The surfboard or contact pressure is a personal preference but I would highly recommend a combination of both. Do not deviate with what has worked in the past. This is not an experiment so I wouldn't treat it as such. As this occurs, the driver may hear slight mumbling and even praying. As red lights continue to occur, as is the case in many scenarios, uttering the phrase, please, please, just get me there, is not out of the question.

As you're deep into Defcon 3, you begin to limit any extra-curricular physical activity that may disturb the lower region. Your time may be limited and the movement could potentially speed up the process. The longer you can stay out of Defcon 4 greatly decreases the chances of your visit with Defcon 5.

Mentally you realize that this particular situation could escalate quite rapidly if any sudden or wrong moves are taken. At any given time you could leapfrog Defcons and ultimately skip one. Very rarely do you ever reverse, especially after you're deep into any Defcon. Don't be fooled and don't let your guard down, reversals are a rarity. You simply get a moderate reprieve or the pain stops momentarily. Trust me, it will return at an alarming rate and even more painful.

Just the thought of knowing you're close to a toilet seems to relax your mind but does nothing for you physically. Your thoughts are racing, What if I don't make it? Why are we hitting every red light? Why did the driver just pass a place with a restroom? You are either praying out loud or quietly to a higher power and that will vary on the company surrounding you.

Physically, the sweat is very noticeable, summer or winter doesn't matter, someone turned on your internal oven and you are burning up inside. Your contractions are pouring in at intervals of 15-30 seconds and the pain, on many occasions is worth doubling over. Of course, doubling over is out of the question because at that point your buttock muscles would relax and that may transport you instantly to Defcon 5 and beyond to the clean-up stage. Your body posture is as tight as a drum. There is no smiling and no small talk. You're quite apprehensive to force any bodily motion that could trigger unwanted internal movement. Segment 2, titled **Walking Powder Keg**, describes several body postures you will encounter in this Defcon.

Mentally at this juncture, you are seriously physically and mentally drained. Hopefully, you've reached the general vicinity where all relief is possible but in your mind, you know that with one wrong move, it could all be over. If Defcon 4 is a common theme in your life, you know every restaurant, store, or general location that has a restroom, how many stalls they have, how busy they are, and if they are for public or private use. You've calculated the percentages time and time again either through success or failure.

At this point, you may begin some prep work. This involves the surety that your belt is easily unhooked or your sweat pants are not knotted. If you're in a vehicle you may have problems exiting due to the movement. A suggestion for your exit is to rotate both legs at one time toward the door. If you exit one leg at a time, this greatly reduces the amount of pressure you're able to maintain in the lower region, and then a *squeesher* hits among other things out of nowhere. As you get deeper into Defcon 4 and a vehicle is something you have to contend with, you may have to quickly exit so you can better control your physical movements. As you exit the vehicle and continue to move forward, there may be times when you have to stop and allow contractions to subside. The time between contractions is critical for moving and making up ground on movement toward relief. When doing so take every precaution to not un-flex your buttock muscles. All of this varies on your past experience while in the Defcon 4 stage. You must know your limitations.

Whether you're the driver or passenger, all parking restrictions are lifted, it's all fair game. There is no empty parking space that is exempt from being filled, no matter what is posted to include expecting mothers, veterans, the president of the company, and employee of the month; EVERYTHING is open season as you move closer to the area of relief.

DEFCON 4.5   "great escape"

Defcon 4.5 has a different feel to it than all the other Defcons. This is a personal accomplishment, one that is felt and told with a sense of pride and is accompanied by a certain tone that touches on beating the odds, hence the name, "the great escape." It is more personal to you and a greater challenge than many couldn't imagine. Simply put, this is one episode, one moment, one trek to the toilet or relief area, one cycle through the Defcons, one instance where you can almost guarantee that Defcon 5 is going to happen and somehow, someway, you escape the drudgery of the one unfortunate circumstance.

Many times this can begin in a vehicle because a great deal of movement is required to exit and involves your lower extremities. So many things are running through your mind, for example, how can I explain this if Defcon 5 hits, can I relieve myself somehow right here? Then through some miracle from above, you find that perfect body posture to maintain reasonable movement and this allows you to break away from the vehicle and begin moving toward your relief location. Meanwhile, you still believe the potential to reach Defcon 5 is extremely plausible, unlike any other time.

Remember, you can go through many Defcons many times and you will, but Defcon 4.5 is saved for that one escape you never thought would be possible. The realization of a Defcon 4.5 isn't confirmed until the relief of the deposit happens anywhere besides your pants. Please note that 4.5 reliefs can occur anywhere and everything is fair game.

Keep in mind, great escapes can outdo each other. They are replaceable but only one can remain titled "the great escape." When you tell someone you experienced a Defcon 4.5, they will know that you have been through a traumatic and mind-blowing journey.

DEFCON 5 congrat "you've arrived"

If you've reached this stage then you're quite aware that "it's time" and "the great escape" have not been fair to you. The final Defcon has unleashed its' tainted fury. You've arrived but not exactly the way you wanted to end this.

Here is a precursor to Defcon 5 hitting.....it's as if you're full steam ahead on the titanic and someone yells iceberg, and you're only 50 yards away and there's no time to change course. It's inevitable that if any release does occur and Defcon 5 has started, it's a rarity that it can be stopped. It's full throttle and the dam has broken. There may be one exception to stopping it, it's a rare feat but it could occur. If during a release, you encounter an air pocket and you're fortunate enough to flex at that very instant. Aside from that, you may as well just let it go and manage the scene after the crash.

17

Even though Defcon 5 greeted and hugged you like your worst enemy, on some demented or twisted level, all the anguish of planning and making it to a place of relief is over. The contractions, cramping, the stress of moving, the pressure and heat waves have stopped, your muscles are now relaxed, they're tired and worn out from flexing and all the close calls, well ....it's all over. The journey has ended. You made it to the Superbowl and lost by a field goal in overtime.

Mentally and physically, on some twisted level, you're relieved that the fight is over. Instant relief has occurred, just not where you want it. Now it's as if a blockbuster movie release has hit the theaters, you're the star and the first to arrive. As you peer around the area, everyone you've invited is standing behind you waiting to see you, that's what this feels like. You've arrived, front and center, all eyes are on you and you have no idea what to do. You're like a deer caught in the headlights, you've gone speechless and your mind is racing with thoughts. There's no way out of this. Depending on your location, you begin to ponder such things as how you will ever live this down, everyone knows, why does this happen to me? I'm sure they can see the stain in my pants. I know their sense of smell had to be alerted by now. You blame the driver for going slow and not making that one critical green light.

There are so many twists and turns but not one instance can define why this happened. It could've been a variety of reasons such as your fateful decision to leave an area too soon where an opportunity for relief could've happened; the gas station with no public restrooms; having no emergency restroom items in your car; rush hour traffic; the famous, "I can hold it just 5 more minutes" or that moment you unconsciously un-flexed the lower region. All you know is your pants are full and you have to deal with it here and now.

Or, you could be alone when Defcon 5 hits and no one will ever know. Either way, the clean-up is never pleasant.

SEGMENT 2
WALKING POWDER KEG

As you become completely aware and intimate with your current situation, the next hurdle is making it to the building or final place of deposit. This requires one thing that is not productive or conducive to your cause and it's simply this…..body movement!!!!

Envision yourself as a **walking powder keg**, there's movement, but the wrong move, bump, twist, turn, jolt, bend, attempt to pass gas, even a sneeze or cough, could be disastrous. Due to the required movement of the lower extremities, if you're exiting a vehicle it must be properly timed and calculated in conjunction with the right body posture so as not to completely disrupt the powder keg. This type of maneuver may require a combination of strategy and body contortion in conjunction with the timing of contractions. Once you've exited the vehicle there are many variations of body movements that could take place. You could also become a walking powder keg in mid stride simply trying to get from one place to another. Here we will explore a few popular methods of walking that just may prevent your visit with Defcon 5.

PEG LEG

The *peg leg* is probably the most popular method of travel while walking. *Peg leg* is walking with one straight leg while the other leg bends to make the move forward possible. It's an opportunity that allows you security in the form of keeping your lower region muscles tight and reducing the risk of a potential escape in that region. This is not a fast move but a move that can be disguised and effective. For example, grabbing your lower back and pretending to have pain in that area is preventing you from walking in a normal fashion, this is one possibility that can disguise this walk. Steps may be your biggest obstacle with this walk. At this point I wouldn't really be too worried what other people think. You're on a mission.

PENGUIN SHUFFLE

The *penguin shuffle* is effective and in some cases can be used inconspicuously if done properly. This is walking with both butt cheeks tightly secured and having to bend your knees at the same time and moving (gliding) at a moderate pace. This can be challenging because your feet will be pointed slightly outward. Your midsection will be slight protruded forward but not enough to be visibly noticeable. However, given that you wore loose pants and a long shirt that covers most of your lower half, this can be pulled off with relative ease. This method is the closest possibility to a natural walk. You can fall into this walk with relative ease and feel comfortable.

MANNEQUIN

If you've ever been to Las Vegas or any other major city with a popular strip, then you have most likely witnessed those who stand perfectly still for hours. You throw some change in their hat and you're in absolute amazement.

Rewind yourself and recall when you were *peg-legging* it to a gas station restroom and a contraction hits hard and all of a sudden, BAM, you had to stop dead in your tracks. You just became that *mannequin* on the strip, except there's no hat to collect money and no one is in amazement. The real problem occurs when you're in someone's path and you are asked to move. Now you have to wait for a contraction to subside to even think about moving. This stoppage can be accompanied by the usage of a phantom phone call or simply stopping to look at your phone. It's simply a prop used by many to provide a valid excuse for any *mannequin* episodes.

If you suddenly have to stop in the middle of a parking lot or entranceway, you hope someone doesn't ask you to move, it could be all over at that point. Of course, movement may occur if you crank up your muscles and switch from *mannequin* to *peg leg* or *penguin shuffle*. This involves a great deal of concentration and focus

22

and must be done very quickly. Running is strictly out of the question but fast walk/shuffling between contractions is a possibility.

TOE CURLING

This may be the most unnoticed natural action you will undertake. It's as if you don't notice it until you find it a nuisance to walk. Toe curling is an automatic, uncontrollable, natural reflex to help you manage the circumstance. You'll eventually notice it when you've stopped or are closer to your relief point.

At the end of the day, no one pays attention to your *peg leg*, *penguin shuffle or mannequin posture*, they're just trying to get through their own day.

My advice to you is this; do the moonwalk if you have to, don't be concerned about what others see or how they question your odd behaviors. Your main objective is to make sure you get relief in the immediate near future.

*HIGH RISK MOVEMENT

During the course of the many journeys you will take part in, inevitably you will encounter a high-risk movement area. These particular areas do not require a hard hat or the possibility of minor or severe injury. They do however require delicate and deliberate movement. The best option is to try and avoid these areas at all costs while in the late stages of Defcon 3 and the entire Defcon 4 stage.

Here are a few areas I would consider avoiding if possible due to the complexity of the landscape. Movement within these areas can disrupt muscle dexterity, thereby leaving you vulnerable to unfortunate circumstances.

*STEPS

At the Defcon 4 stage, this will be your biggest obstacle and the most unavoidable. The key to working steps is to try and reduce the total number to less than 3. I understand this is practically impossible. Your passage through this unwanted area can be done without major affect if you simply work around stomach cramps and contractions. This can be done by the use of deliberate movement between the shards of pain. The lower rear muscles have to work at full maximum ability if you are going to tackle more than 3 steps. One possible way to make this an easier transition is to simply take one step at a time by simply doing so between contractions.

*PEOPLE

Yes, people are on the list and for good reason…they can potentially impede movement. If you're in a crowd of people, this will seriously reduce your delicate and deliberate motion as well as increase the time you manage a Defcon 4 stage. People are not watching you and they're certainly not aware of your situation. The parting of the Red Sea is not in your immediate future so prepare yourself for some strategic bobbing and weaving.

Pretend as if you're an NFL running back in slow motion. This could potentially take place at large events such as concerts, amusement parks, festivals, fairs, an indoor or outdoor mall, and even a crowded restaurant or a popular bar.

*UNEVEN TERRAIN/HILLS

You ask yourself, where will I encounter this? Several places may include a golf course, your movement to and through woods in search of cover and concealment, or your own front or backyard. Hills with a steep or slight grade could cause variable body posturing that is not conducive to your end goal. Traveling in such areas could cause some serious issues.

*PASSENGER VEHICLE/SUV/TRUCK

I realize these are unavoidable, but here's the reality of it all. Most unfortunate circumstances will be the result of entry and exit from your mode of transportation. The primary danger zone is at the threshold of the door. Your timing, speed, and mode of movement are critical in this area. You have to be simultaneously delicate and deliberate. There can be no hesitation with movements and leg transfer. Make no mistake; Defcon 5 will happen almost instantly if your calculations are the slightest bit off. It doesn't matter your location or how close you are to your relief point, you can be in your driveway, and it doesn't matter. Defcon 5 doesn't discriminate against any person, location, or any circumstances whatsoever.

SEGMENT 3
YOU HAVE OPTIONS...DON'T PANIC

In Segment 3, we will look at a *Defcon artist's* breakdown of relief areas. Many would consider such uncommon areas of relief to be obscure but at the end of the day, there is no such thing as an uncommon area. There are very few places of relief that is out of the question or frowned upon. The only thing that may alter the usage of an area is the lack of cover and concealment.

TOILET AVAILABILITY IQ (TA-IQ)

The most underestimated and overlooked part of your journey is your *"Toilet Availability IQ"* (TA-IQ). TA-IQ is not complicated; it's your knowledge of the most opportune areas for relief. Of course, if you're a veteran *Defcon artist*, this will certainly not be an issue. If you're a novice or an infrequent flyer, this can potentially be your ultimate downfall. There will always be glitches, unforeseen circumstances and of course, Murphy's Law will generally find its way into the equation. Keep in mind, none of the locations I provide below are foolproof, just a loose guide to assist you on your journey. For example, there are certain things you can reasonably predict either locally or beyond your playground. Sometimes we have

27

to stray from the standard area of relief and branch out due to absolute necessity. This is primarily based on your current Defcon stage as well as the severity of how quickly you're moving through each stage. Here are two of the most popular places to visit.

FAST FOOD RESTAURANTS
(low availability/moderate cleanliness)
This is a low percentage go-to for usage, and for good reason. Most restaurants only have one stall and they're in high demand and usage. Keep in mind, their usage is not simply from patrons but also travelers. It's quick and easy and directly off the interstate. A true sit-down restaurant has a higher percentage of availability. They're equipped with more than one stall and generally their usage by patrons or travelers isn't that frequent in comparison to fast food restaurants.

GAS STATIONS / CONVENIENCE STORES
(moderate availability/low cleanliness)
Here's where it gets tricky. When you're dealing with the unknown outside of your zip code or backyard this can create havoc and stress. Some States require public restroom availability at gas stations, and others do not. Gas stations and convenience stores are generally coupled together. The stores that do not offer fuel generally do not have public restrooms and you

may consider them as the standard "mom and pop" locations.

The usage of a restroom in a true "mom and pop" convenience store is a rarity, especially if it is privately owned. The only way you may be able to gain usage is to have a serious look and a voice of desperation and quite honestly, that generally means absolutely nothing in their world. Your first thought is, I just want to drop my pants here and deposit on their floor. Your second thought is your question to them, where do you go to the bathroom? An option could be usage around the back of the store if it provides cover and concealment and no cameras. Your time is expiring and you may have no choice because getting back in that car is going to require a mandatory meeting with Defcon 5.

If you pull off usage in a true privately owned convenience store then you've done some serious convincing and I congratulate you on a job well done. Pulling this off could be the difference between ending at a Defcon 3 or 5.

The restrooms inside the gas stations are generally designated for men and women and they're stand-alone (one person at a time). If you're at or above a Defcon 3 at this stage of the game, because Defcons can leapfrog ahead or progress at a rapid pace, you must find an area for relief sooner than later. No matter what gender you are, if your restroom gender is locked, simply knock and tug on the other door. If it's open, GO….lock the door behind you and do your business. The dirty look you might receive when you leave means absolutely nothing when you consider what is at stake.

Always remember…..*You play the Defcons, don't let the Defcons play you. Stay in control and stay one step ahead of the game.*

OUTSIDE THE BOX USAGE

 TA-IQ is acquired over time and thinking outside the box can many times be your saving grace. Here are a few recommendations and tips for relief usage.

CONSTRUCTION SITE
(moderate availability/very low cleanliness)
These areas are generally equipped with a port-a-potty. I would not stop to ask anyone's permission; too much time is involved in searching for the right person. You will generally have to walk through unsafe areas and it's not worth the risk. You also run the risk of someone saying "no" (not sure who would say no but there's always one). These are dudes on a construction site, I'm pretty sure they understand your dilemma.

Quick tip on this relief location: When utilizing a port-a-potty you must consider one thing, **backsplash**. One way to prevent backsplash is to cover the top of the toilet seat with toilet paper. Extend it across the open area so the opening is completely covered. Here you are going to use the *Drone* method (described in Segment 5). This does put you at a higher drop distance and it may seem that the potential for backsplash is higher but the cover you placed on the toilet lid takes the backsplash out of the equation.

HOTEL LOBBY

(high availability/very high cleanliness)

If you have a choice this is your best bet based on the probability of usage and cleanliness. It's the perfect spot. Generally, patrons use their hotel room bathroom so the lobby is generally wide open. The trick to using these restrooms hinges on your ability to be deliberate and act like you've been there before. As a rule, no one will question why you're there, and do whatever you can to avoid asking the location of a restroom. You should know it's either to the left or right on the ground floor. If you ask you run the risk of being shut out by a "rule stickler." The word "no" is not an option at this point.

FRIEND or RELATIVE

Don't underestimate these locations. Trust me, when your back is against the wall this will seem like a genius move. It's either that or you face an unfortunate circumstance that you would rather not partake in for many obvious reasons. It's a moderately safe area and critically important to know if anyone is home before you arrive at these locations. If they're not home there's always the radical move of their backyard. I know it's crazy but consider the alternative. You have to know two things, are they home? and what's the cover and concealment of the area?

WOODS - ANY ROADWAY

Are you stuck in bumper-to-bumper traffic or with minimal movement on the interstate and there are woods next to you? If so, you're in luck, just don't forget the handful of napkins you took from the fast food restaurant. Make sure that you have good cover and concealment because in standstill traffic people have nothing to do except watch what's happening around them. Woods can also be utilized on roads in rural areas. These areas are a far distance from civilization and your journey through the Defcons shows no mercy.

BUSINESS OFFICE
(high cleanliness/high availability)
Great option if you know the location is within close proximity because they are not always clearly marked. Sometimes your attire will dictate this usage but unless you're dressed like you've lived on the streets for weeks, you should be good to go. Be aware that some business offices may have a security department overseeing the area and of course you have to ask them. It's hard to imagine them saying "no" but just in case don't forget to give a desperate look and voice of concern.

GROCERY or DEPARTMENT STORE
(moderate cleanliness & availability)
A low to mid-range usage area for a couple reasons: the parking may be too far away from the entrance and unless you know the store layout, the restrooms could be in the back of the store. It's a challenge to *peg leg* or *penguin shuffle* to the back of the store but of course that all varies on your level of desperation.

*ROLL OF THE DICE

There will be certain locations where the possibility for relief is possible but dicey, so keep in mind these locations can be a crap shoot. In all reality, anything outside the normal bathroom/restroom with the standard toilet has the potential to bring forth unusual occurrences.

YOUR HOME

Yes, this is on the list and can be hit or miss as you factor in this scenario. It's your turn to host Thanksgiving dinner and you've invited 17 of your friends and relatives. At some point toward the end of dinner or shortly thereafter, you may need a ticket taker for the one bathroom that's available in your ranch home because the basement isn't finished and the rough-in is not complete. When this event occurs, do yourself a favor, locate a spot in your backyard and utilize the 5-gallon bucket for your usage in your garage. You frown on this now, but wait until you're standing outside your own bathroom at Defcon 4 and then this won't be such an obscure idea. Remember, all is fair and reasonable when you consider the alternative.

INSIDE A DUMPSTER ENCLOSURE

Tread lightly in this area. This is very unpredictable due to the random usage of visits by restaurant or store personnel. The only safe time for usage is after hours but you have to insure three things are in order: the enclosure is unlocked (if it has doors), there are no vehicles in the lot (just because they are closed doesn't mean someone isn't inside cleaning) and lastly, be observant of pole cameras facing toward the inside of the enclosure.

GOLF COURSE

Pack the moist wipes in your golf bag and I guarantee they will come in handy. The golf course is hit or miss and is based solely on hole location and the amount of woods surrounding the area. It also depends on your distance from the clubhouse. If woods are within reasonable walking distance and there's good cover and concealment, you're in business. You don't want that foursome of older ladies peering at you. If the clubhouse is a better option and closer, you better get on it. Whatever is in the cart stays, you have no time to ask your buddy or anyone in your foursome if they need anything, just get in and go.

This situation is most likely to occur when you make the turn because those two hot dogs or cheeseburgers will hit you around holes 11 or 12.

AIRCRAFT

This is a rarity but due to the location and potential circumstances and outcome, it is valuable information to take into consideration. If you find yourself in this predicament you must account for a couple things. Be observant of movement in the cabin about who is getting out of their seat to use the restroom. Do not panic at this point because the probability of long term usage is unlikely.

One thing you should be concerned with most on an aircraft involves the distribution of drinks and snacks. In this case, all movement toward any restroom is completely out of the question. You can't even fit a sheet of paper between the cart and the seats. The chance of you getting anywhere is not happening. Do yourself a favor and do a body check before drink and snack process begins. Be aware of even the slightest amount of cramping, discomfort or gas. Getting out of any aircraft seat does not help your cause and could easily propel you into higher Defcons.

*LAST RESORT

Here are few items to consider keeping in your vehicle just in case you're blindsided by Defcon 4:

- ➤ **1 roll of toilet paper - 1 pack of moist wipes**
- ➤ **5-gallon bucket with a lid, large tarp, bedpan**

The items listed are for an absolute last resort option, call it plan Z. Plan Z is a foolproof option for relief. These items will allow you to produce a makeshift area for relief and here's how.

Park your vehicle in an area that has an extremely mild flow of traffic. Park so one side is directed away from an area where other vehicles enter or exit. On the side away from traffic, open both doors and proceed to drape the tarp over the both doors and make sure it's close to the ground on all sides. Utilize the 5-gallon bucket and the moist wipes and there you have it…relief. At this point, you can complete your deposit and/or release the first wave if needed to allow yourself enough time for the next potential second wave or a traditional setting.

Do not underestimate the potential usage of the bedpan. The next time you're in the hospital make sure one leaves with you. Stash the pan in a bag and take it home with you. You will be surprised that one day when that one incident occurs it will come in handy. Keep that in your trunk in a bag out of site.

SEGMENT 4
10 SECONDS TO HEAVEN OR HELL

 During each stage of particular Defcons, there is no time that is more critical than the 10 seconds you will spend moving through the restroom and into your stall. Those 10 seconds are bottled up between the time you place your hand on the restroom door until such time that you are safe and secure seated comfortably on your throne.

As you pull the main restroom door, your senses and hypervigilance are off the charts. Your sense of sight, hearing, and smell are on full alert. Upon completing your first and second step into the restroom, your eyes shift immediately to the stall area. Urinals are obsolete and completely overlooked. Your focus is on the stall region. You are looking for feet on the floor, a cracked stall door, a child waiting for his father, any type of noise emitting from that area, a slightly ajar door, how many stalls are there, and how many people are standing in line?

As you move closer and glide across the floor, you are listening for any movement inside the stall. As a rule, many people will emit noise from a stall indicating that someone is in there. It could be in the form of a clearing of the throat or a fake lackluster cough. If intentional noises are emitted from the stall, it is generally a signal to back off, do not open the door because if the latch has the slightest give, the current user is going to be upset. The entire time you are inconspicuously using your sense of smell, you just never want to display it.

You're about 5 seconds into the walk and your senses have not alerted to anything that would lead you to believe anyone is using at least one of the stalls that you so desperately need because Defcon 4 is about to reach its full maximum capacity.

The back-and-forth mental anguish, the physical pain and torture, slow and fast driving, the red lights, comments from the passenger(s), the passage of Defcon 4.5, the praying, curse words, mumbling, the awkward walks, and the concentration it took to get here are wrapped up in the last one or two seconds. The moment of truth doesn't occur until that stall door handle you pull, actually opens. When it opens it's like heaven and if it's locked, well........you're shit out of luc

SEGMENT 5
WHERE ALL THE MAGIC HAPPENS

When the time does occur and you're in the restroom inside that grey box unscathed and secluded from the real world, or so it seems, you will begin to experience a multitude of events or personal happenings that can just amaze you. Your main objective has been met, you've escaped Defcon 5. Here we will look at the events that occur within your subleased grey box. The experiences may completely baffle the novice but for an experienced *Defcon Artists*, it's just another day at the office. For each encounter or circumstance, I've created quick reference names for easy identification.

MOVE ON, NOTHING TO SEE HERE

The grey box you're occupying and temporarily leasing is sacred ground and no trespassing is allowed. Due to the potential weakness of your leased property, a broken lock, weak or lose fittings, and hair-trigger lock mechanisms, your level of security is always at risk. Therefore, when a new person arrives in the restroom you create noise to let them know you are occupying this stall. This form of claiming your box may be a slight cough; a ruffling of papers, or a flush of the toilet, either way, your stall is accounted for, so BACK OFF.

DON'T ASSUME ANYTHING

As you're standing outside the stall waiting patiently, you may hear the toilet flush. It's easy to assume the person is finished, but hold on, you hear nothing further to indicate that to be true. There is no follow-up roll of toilet paper and no rustling or movement inside, it's as quiet as a church mouse. What you're experiencing is a *courtesy flusher*.

A *courtesy flusher* will flush for various reasons. It could be after each deposit because they're courteous; they may not want everyone to hear an actual deposit or they're simply reducing the potential odor that could occur. Never assume anyone is finished until you're standing in the stall.

LAYING THE GROUNDWORK

The groundwork is simply this....on your way to the stall and before you enter you have taken the time to undo all necessary buttons, 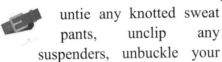 untie any knotted sweat pants, unclip any suspenders, unbuckle your belt, and depending on the severity you may have gone so far as to unbutton the pants and pull down your zipper as you grasp the front of your pants to prevent them from falling. Its crunch time and it's a matter of inches and seconds as you're within several feet of relief. Keep in mind, the laying of the groundwork could start as early as needed, like your vehicle. Don't assume it should only begin inside the restroom.

THE ENCORE

Just as any good rock band performs an encore, so do you. After your relief occurs, you're all cleaned up; you stand up and realize you have to go again. You're a bit frustrated but you knew it was probably inevitable based on the pressure below. You return to the stage for round two, it's a short stint and generally does the trick.

THE DANCE

You've arrived and by all accounts you're going to make it. You're so happy that you've arrived 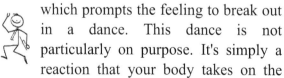 which prompts the feeling to break out in a dance. This dance is not particularly on purpose. It's simply a reaction that your body takes on the closer you get to the stall. The full dance routine is on display directly in front of the toilet, inside the stall. You're in private mode so any crazy moves are yours and yours only. Keep in mind, you may unknowingly either mumble or speak out loud during the dance.

PICASO

These are rare occasions but this can and will occur across all spectrums from a novice to Defcon artists. As you squat and clear the rear area with your pants, there may be a time when you prematurely relax the lower region and unknowingly begin to relieve yourself before actually connecting your flesh to the seat. This may result in the release of a high-velocity projectile. As a result, the wall and the toilet will take a portion of the projectile. For a brief moment, you may feel bad for the store owner but that moment generally subsides within a few seconds because you're just happy to get relief. The clean-up is quick and as effective as possible. A quick escape is the main objective at this point. Your hope is that the coast is clear when you exit the area and no eyes are on you during the escape.

If you should be unfortunate enough to pass someone going in as you're coming out, a little white lie never hurt anyone. It should go something like this, "I'm not sure who was in there but they left it a mess.

READY….SET….GO

There is a moment in time when you finally reach the toilet and you find yourself doing nothing, you're not dancing, you're not even speaking or mumbling, all you're doing is praying and staring at the stall with your back to the toilet. You're frozen in time simply because any movement downward or any bend at the waist could be disastrous. Every second counts, so please know that even inside the stall, Defcon 5 can even sneak one in there even when you thought you were safe. You're locked tight, standing with your feet and legs as close together as humanly possible with your toes curled.

One of two things eventually will occur at this point. A contraction needs to subside and then the possibility of bending is an option. If a contraction does not subside then plan B is in order. Plan B is very tricky and not foolproof. You must be somewhat athletic and quick to pull this off. The percentages are not on your side if the contraction doesn't subside. You must be able to pull off a simultaneous pull down (pants) and squat at the same time and know that when you release, there will be a high percentage that your release will be before your skin hits the toilet seat. Just hope the percentage is enough that most, if not all, hits the water. If

45

not, then refer to *PICASO* and that will be your outcome.

CANNONBALL

When a cannonball occurs it is not something you care to brag about or refer back to at any point during your hilarious sharing sessions. A cannonball occurs when a small amount of air is released, and then it's as if a wad of extract is shot from the lower region at a very high velocity. It's a fast and hard shot that makes dropping the kids off at the pool seem like child's play. In this instance, you're not dropping them off; you're violently throwing them into the pool. The result is a splash that will send chills up your spine from the toilet water. Let your short term memory go away and forget about that the moment it happens.

DROP DEAD LEGS

We've all been there, sitting for a long period of time and your leg circulation is cut off by the configuration of the toilet seat. Before you know it, both legs are completely numb, and standing at this point is not an option. You must first maneuver your legs in a position to take pressure off and allow blood flow. Then and only then can you even begin to think about standing.

NIAGARA

This is probably the most self-explanatory activity within the group. It's simply a small version of a fire hydrant being turned on from inside your body. It can be violent and traumatic at times and seem never-ending. *NIAGARA* and *THE ENCORE* go hand in hand. Of course, *NIAGARA* is the prerequisite to *THE ENCORE* and this session could last a reasonable amount of time depending on the severity of the sickness and the number of *ENCORES* you're going to give.

ARE YOU SERIOUS?

This requires one sign and one sign only, "no public restrooms available" or "restroom out of order." There's nothing to explain here except your Defcon 3 just turned into Defcon 4 by simply reading the sign. The game plan definitely changes.

YOU'RE GLUE-TON FOR PUNISHMENT

Just when you thought the human body couldn't produce a glue-like substance…. think again. Whatever just came out felt like I recently ate a bottle of white pasty glue for dinner. The hard part is just beginning, getting all that glue off and only using a half roll of toilet paper. You could sure use some handy moist wipes right about now. The wipe is never ending and it's followed up with a few choice words of disbelief.

DRONE

Many times when you enter the stall area you will encounter the yellow beaded toilet seat. We all know the prior visitor was either a 10-year-old or a male adult too lazy to lift. Here we're engaged in the drone position which is "basic hovering 101," a common posture in any and all port-a-pottys. Due to the awkward posture of the *DRONE*, you don't want to spend more time than absolutely necessary in that position. If the *DRONE* position is held too long and the leg burn sets in just hope there is a handicapped railing next to the toilet to keep your balance. Due to the distance from the seat, the likelihood of a backsplash is minimal. Be careful on the initial deposit, this position provides the greatest percentage and probability of a *PICASO* happening.

GENDER.....WHAT GENDER?

This is what many would call an Omaha, an audible that can only work in a so-called penny or single defense. A penny or single defense is your standalone restroom. You enter, lock the door and you're alone, gender at that point is meaningless, you have the toilet and that's all that matters. Local gas stations are notorious for them. Here you enter the store with the penguin shuffle so you know it's serious. The restrooms are side by side. At this point, there is zero hesitation. You knock on your gender's door and it's locked. You knock on the other gender and it's unlocked. There should be zero hesitation, get in there. There's no questions asked, an audible took place and the rest is history. You may get a look on the way out but who cares, you won.

CLIFFHANGER

The end of your session has arrived and your one final deposit has occurred…...or has it? You have that feeling that one final dropping has yet to fall but instincts tell you that something is lingering. This is accompanied and verified by a small shake, a slight but ever-increased side-to-side motion that will drop that cliffhanger that you can assuredly guarantee is there. The side-to-side motion could occur more than once but generally speaking, a quick final shake confirms your suspicion and it's off the hook. You're now free to continue.

SWIRLED PYTHON

It just keeps going and going and going. This gets its name from both the look and length. This is very self-explanatory and visually an easy target to identify. You have one question you have as you stand and briefly observe, I hope this toilet doesn't clog u

OUT OF SIGHT, OUT OF MIND

You've arrived, deposited and unleashed a Texas Wall Mounter. All of this has been done outside the home and for that you're thankful. Upon completion, you stand in awe and quickly realize…there's no way I can flush this without causing mild flooding to the area. Maybe...just maybe, you'll feel bad for 5 to 10 seconds because you know someone is going to have to manage this cleanup. After 10 seconds are up and you're outside that door, nothing else matters except you're back and you're ready to face and defeat another round of Defcons.

I'M OUTTA HEAR

You're sitting comfortably on the throne and for purpose of completion; this session could basically be over. You're only waiting because you feel a slight pressure and just want to make sure a mild second wave isn't lurking in the background. At this particular time you are playing on your cell phone and someone enters a restroom stall. Shortly thereafter, that person creates and you hear one of the most horrific sounds. At this point, any thoughts of waiting for the second wave has been abandoned and cleared from the plan. It's as if you called an Omaha. You cringe at the noise with a mild disgust and can't get out of there fast enough. Due to your fleet footed movement, the odor never had a chance to catch up with you.

HANDI...WHAT?

There are occasions when some rules and directed signage do not apply to you and if questioned you can certainly justify the disobedience. For example, if you're approaching or deeply rooted in a Defcon 3 and quickly approaching a 4, parking spaces or restroom stalls that are designated for certain persons are the least of your concern and all are fair game for usage. A parking ticket and/or a look of disgust are a small price to pay for the potential damage that could potentially occur. This goes for designated parking spaces that may include handicapped parking, employee of the month, expecting mothers, veterans, and/or Chief of Police just to name a few. On rare occasion a fire lane may come into play and you'll know because Defcon 5 is loudly trying to knock down your door.

VIP LIST

You have a group in your phone contacts that you may be aware of or you may not. This list involves incoming calls only. On occasion, depending on the necessity; you may have to make an outgoing call. This VIP List is comprised of the person(s) that you will accept a phone call while sitting in your grey box. After about 15 to 20 seconds into the conversation you'll generally be asked the question, "it sounds like you're in a tunnel" or "what's that echo?" For those on your VIP list, you have no hesitation or qualms telling those in the selected group what is happening and you're your location. Inevitably someone is going to flush a toilet and your cover is blown. By the way, there's no such thing as whispering in a restroom. No matter how low you talk, it will be heard.

HEAD ON COLLISION

This pertains to guys only. The sit down happens and as comfortable seating is taking place, you are suddenly overtaken by a small chill up and down your spine coupled with a slight touch of coolness directly in front of you. This is the direct result of a particular body part making a direct head-on collision with the inside of the white porcelain. Your body position is quickly redirected, all contact is disengaged and thoughts of what just happened can't escape your thoughts quick enough. A few minor thoughts run through your mind, and you know what they are, but it's back to business as usual.

CONSTI POO TION

You're in your gray box, everything is working like a well-oiled machine and then it's as if a damn was immediately constructed or everyone went out walked off the job in the lower region. All production has stopped, nothing is getting through, the union has called for a strike and there's a lull in the gunfire. You sit in bewilderment and wonder what just happened. In the next several moments you sit quietly waiting for movement, anything to indicate production will begin again but the jury is still out. This is the moment when you ever so lightly hold your breath and push. Before you know it you are on the verge of busting a blood vessel or so it seems.

Eventually, one of two things is going to occur and busting a blood vessel is not one of them. Either the pushing aided in the movement or you eventually just say, "forget it" wait for the next relief moment to occur. On the rare occasion when you stand you could experience a breakthrough or an *encore*, but it's highly unlikely.

An advanced option or technique is to move your middle torso in a circular motion while sitting on the toilet. You can throw in a stand up, sit down and a bend forward option for good measure. This is called "toilet gymnastics" and could potentially allow for intestinal movement. This is an advanced move so give it a try and it may do the trick.

MAJOR BREAKTHROUGH

One-ply, two-ply, three-ply, four….. What does that mean? Absolutely nothing except that no matter how many plys your toilet tissue may be, a finger breakthrough will occur at some point. It's an unpleasant feeling and sheer desperation to clean has overtaken the relief session. Everything from this point forward is done with caution when touching something.

HOLD ON, WHAT DID YOU SAY?

On occasion, there may be a moment when a verbal exchange happens between you and the grey box next to you. This is not out of the question if this does occur; just know that anything beyond standard dude talk may be subject to scrutiny. Here are a few occasions and only a few where you may feel comfortable. You definitely know your friend is next to you OR someone asks for toilet paper because they are out and you oblige because what comes around goes around. Even at that point, it's a quick flip or roll of the paper and small talk generally doesn't follow that exchange

Don't talk to me

TIME OUT

When you walk into this particular restroom it's rather quiet with no traffic and 2 empty stalls. When you enter the lights automatically turn on. You don't give it much thought so you move forward to occupy a stall. Due to the peacefulness, you take the extra time to go three more levels on one of your cellphone games. As you finish the level all of a sudden the lights go out, it's pitch black.

Your first initial thought is someone turned the lights out and her comes the chainsaw massacre. After 5-10 seconds, reality sets in and you realize the lights have sensors. The lights have timed out and the massacre quickly fades from thought. In order to get these lights back on you're going to need to stand and wave your arms. Your objective is to stand and wave your arms. On occasion, you may have to open the stall door and extend your arms.

NO TP

This outcome can go either way, difficult or easy. It all depends on the location, how many stalls are present and more importantly are they occupied. This will happen numerous times before you learn your lesson. The lesson is to check the dispenser or the entire stall for toilet paper. If it's in the dispenser or the back of the toilet, you're golden and take the NO TP out of the equation. If it's a shotgun stall (one stall) and no toilet paper is available you could go into straight panic mode because one of two things could occur. One, you have no time to go ask for TP and secondly, it's the new age restroom and green because it's all air cry. Old school was simple, rip off a huge wad of paper towels and head into your grey box.

SURFACE SUPOSITORY

We all know what a suppository is, its purpose and what it can do. In this particular case, the suppository I have mentioned doesn't enter anything on the body. This particular suppository occurs when direct pressure is applied to the very specific pinpointed release area during the clean-up (wiping) stage. For some unknown reason this triggers a release just as if an actual suppository was used.

Do not get this confused with the *Encore*. Granted, round two is going to happen but for various reasons. The *Encore* is the result of internal colon combustion and in this particular situation only surface pressure is required.

PREEMPTIVE STRIKE

This is can be defined in many ways. The preemptive strike is conducted with the intent of reducing the rigors of the Defcon world from reeking-havoc in your near future. This will most likely happen in the early beginnings of the Defcon 1 stage. It can be defined as a shot in the dark; let's test the waters; nothing to lose and much to gain. Based on experience and that particular feeling, you simply make an attempt to force a deposit. It's not the blood vessel popping serious grunting attempt. It's a casual walk-in restroom attitude with the chance that it might just happen and if it does it can certainly reduce the pressure at a later time.

With the preempted strike you basically take that unfortunate circumstance out of the equation or at least reduce the probability.

TURTLE RACE

This is one of those rare non-emergency trips. The pressure is there but it's a constant push/pull. This is a break from the standard pants on fire rush. This relief only lasts for a few moments and then reality rears its ugly head. As relief begins you start you feel like you shot a starter gun for a turtle race, everything seems to be in slow motion. You find out quickly this is no standard box turtle race. You feel like these are no longer box turtles but a race that involves giant Sulcata Tortoises (90-200 lbs.). The expression on your face from the pain says it all. It is accompanied by light to moderate foot stomping coupled with disbelief. No matter how long it takes, you know you can't pinch this off mid-stride because it's practically impossible to restart. Your best option is to tough it out and roll with it. Maybe a more appropriate comparison to the tortoise is a soft drink 12 ounce can.

LOCKSMITH TO STALL 3 PLEASE

This doesn't happen very often but when it does you're generally in the large stalls where the door is not directly in front of you. I'm talking about a non-existent or broken lock. In a standard stall you're close enough to hold the door with a simple reach. In a larger or handicapped stall you're not so fortunate because the door is generally at a 90 degree from you. You have that feeling like it's on the other side of the world. This is going to require a verbal shout out to someone you think is too close with a high probability of entry. Even if they don't intend to enter you have to at least give the aforementioned warning.

SILENT WAITER

"Waiter" is defined as someone who enters a restroom searching for a stall. They're unseen upon entry due to your position in a stall. The waiter rattles stall doors and fades away within the confines of the restroom, just lingering and waiting for occupancy. They create instant

pressure solely by their physical presence in the same room. Here's a scenario of how this shakes out.

You've just entered a one stall restroom. You waste no time getting seated and the main door opens. Within seconds you feel a tug on your stall   door. At that point you can elect to say something or remain quiet. Just be careful what you say, don't put a time limit on your stay it by saying, "I'll just be a minute." Remember, your minute is a lifetime to someone else who is fighting back the transcendence into Defcon 4.

A few seconds later the main door opens; however, you don't know if the person who tugged on your door left the restroom or a new person arrived. You do hear the urinal being used and shortly thereafter the sink. Moments later, the main door opens again and there you are, in total silence, waiting for a hint of noise from the potential waiter, the pressure cooker. You can definitely hear a pin drop because you just want to know who is in the room. After a few moments you just carry on with business as usual. You do your business quicker than usual due to the pressure.

The two stall restroom is very similar except you arrived after the first stall was occupied and the same scenario occurs. Someone tugs at your door, except this time you just want to shout, "The guy in the first stall was here first, I just sat down."

YOU'RE ON THE CLOCK

You have only been dating a month and you're together at a restaurant or her house watching a movie. Out of nowhere, you immediately go to a Defcon 2 and 3 are approaching rapidly. There is one thing running through your mind, how can I go #2 without her actually knowing I went #2? It's all about timing. How much time can I spend in the bathroom before the standard #1 would've ended? This has to be quick work. This can be accomplished if you just deposit the first wave and go back for round 2 a bit later. If you can pull this off round 2 can be accompanied with a potential excuse such as, I drank too much water.

If you're at a home where you're watching a movie in a basement, we all know that the bathroom is generally within eye and earshot. In this situation you just have to live with the reality of them knowing.

SENSORY OVERLOAD

As you enter the stall area and you actually have time, which can be a rarity, you see the sanitary covers hanging on the wall. They look great and work really well.....when you can keep it in place.

As you pull one from the wall, you place it on the toilet seat and within 3 to 5 seconds, say goodbye to the sanitary cover and hello to a 4 letter word. This is all determined by one feature... the dreaded flush sensor. Every time you place it on the toilet seat and move, the toilet flushes, taking the sanitary cover with it. After round 2 and a few choice words, you either forget it or go old school and use toilet paper to line the seat. The one good thing about the sanitary cover is it does prevent the ***head on collision.***

SEGMENT 6
1 – PLEASE STEP FORWARD

When you enter the restroom for the purpose of going #1 it's a tad bit more toned down, less urgency. When you see stalls you can recall journey and the fight it took to get there? Now you can stand back, relax and watch others scramble their way into the restroom stall peg legging it and praying one is open. You can just laugh all that off as you take joy in knowing it's just "urinal time."

Here we will explore various incidents and behaviors that happen at the restroom urinal.

HAND WARMER

A slight sense of urgency is involved during this visit. A quick fumbling of the zipper takes place one to two steps just prior to the clearing of the threshold. As you begin your release, you're practically looking at the ceiling as you let out a sigh of relief.

Moments later you feel a warm sensation in one of your hands. You know that feeling all too well as you immediately fumble and stop all production to the best of your ability. A slight shaking of the hand is in order and hope that you're not wearing your khaki thin dress pants today.

STRAY CAT

No matter what, there could be 5 urinals with separators, 3 available and one stall with a line. Inevitably a *stray cat* will wait in the line for a stall for #1. Is it stage freight? Is it the awkwardness of another man standing next to you or was there an incident that prompted this reason to isolate? This is not for me to speculate. Carry on *stray cat*, whatever makes you feel comfortable. Refer to *don't be lazy* for a viable reason.

STRAY CAT'S EVIL TWIN

As you enter the restroom for urinal usage you observe 6 urinals with separators and guess what, none of them are occupied. You feel like a rock star, you have the pick of the liter, the urinal of your choice. You elect as many do, the end urinal, the one against the wall. No less than 5 seconds later, no sooner than the zipper is down, another urinal chaser enters the restroom. Your peripheral vision catches what you believe to be a person walking toward you. In the back of your mind you can't imagine that person is going to utilize the urinal next to you when all 5 are wide open, but guess what……he does. You're in total bewilderment and you just have to ask….why? There is no logical answer except maybe this could be *stray cat's evil twin*.

CHOKE HOLD

You already know the knot is there and it's moderately tight. You elect to not undo it because it could take a reasonable amount of time. You're willing to roll the dice on this one.

The approach toward the urinal threshold is somewhat standard except for that step when you have a slight dip forward with your mid-section. This is the result of that untied lace that's screaming as you stretch it farther away from your body. As that is happening you're simultaneously pulling and stretching until a *choke hold* is performed on your two boys. One hand must remain between you and the boys or a severe choking would take place. As you release the *choke hold* don't be so quick to take the boys home. Take the time to release the hold, allow your boys to finish and then take them home. The alternative is the boys will finish no matter if they're outside or in the house.

DON'T BE LAZY

Prior to urinal separators, there was always that one in the crowd that you would experience on occasion. They had the *lazy eye*. There a certain protocol or etiquette that comes with urinal usage. It's a fairly simple process. Walk up to the urinal, unzip or pull down for usage, shake once or twice, send everyone back home, close up shop and move on. During that entire

64

process there is a stance that should be maintained. The stance is simple, your upper torso and feet are facing the urinal in front of you; your head is looking just above the horizon or the sky. Before the urinal separators, the *lazy eye's* stance was a bit off center, their eyes and head was below the horizon and there you have it…the *lazy eye*.

If I had to take a guess, the *stray cat* could very well be the direct result of the *lazy eye* and what that brought to the urinal. I can't say I don't blame them for their movement to the stall.

MAID OF THE MIST
If you're utilizing a urinal that has a sensor, then the *maid of the mist* has played a part in your visit. This will come into play when bodily movement is made in front of the urinal, trips the sensor and the flush are beyond your control. As that occurs, the boys are exposed, still out and experience the *maid of the mist*. Do your business; get the boys back inside and then move around. Don't let that sensor play you.

THE GREAT BARRIER
If there was any one simple addition to the men's restroom that has changed the usage of going # 1 at a urinal, it is definitely the addition of that barrier that separates the urinals. You may not have put too much thought into this but

it has opened and closed so many positive and negative things that could affect your visit to the urinal. Let's take a look at how it has affected your visit pre and post barrier and the positive outcome.

Pre barrier

You had to keep your head at or above the horizon in front of you. This is mentioned in the *lazy eye* segment above.

Post barrier

You are free to look up and down at your leisure. This allows you to eliminate the potential for a *hand warmer.* I still wouldn't stray visually too far right or left; you could appear to be attempting to look over the barrier (not cool). This also allows you to see the advertiser on the urinal cake at the bottom of the urinal. You can also aim at things you want to hit and this could reduce splash back if you hit the wrong thing.

Pre barrier

For the subconscious participants, size mattered.

Post barrier

For any participant, none of that matters. It's just you and the porcelain.

Pre barrier

One, maybe two shakes if needed, no more.

Post barrier

Not that you need more than one or two but just in case you need a couple extra or you're having a few difficulties, shakes could exceed 6 or 7 and no one will ever know. Shake within reason please.

Pre barrier

You can just feel the pressure and the anxiety. According to Better Health Channel, "A person with paruresis (shy bladder syndrome) finds it difficult or impossible to urinate when other people are around. Paruresis is believed to be one of the most common types of social phobia." (2)

Post barrier

I'm not saying this eliminates the phobia but it sure could help resolve some of the factors that brought on the phobia. This barrier could unlock the mental block that paves the road to recovery and addresses any issues that caused it.

SEGMENT 7
DEAD END.....ROAD CLOSED

This segment has stories shared by those who have experienced and traveled through countless Defcon stages and either escaped Defcon 5 in the most obscure places or reached the unfortunate circumstance.

NAKED AND LOST IN A CORN FIELD

It was a warm sunny day and I had one final interview to complete for a police recruit background. This particular interview happened to be 15 miles deep into farm country. As I began my journey in the early afternoon I stopped at a fast food restaurant. It was almost lunchtime and I knew when I completed this interview it would be close to dinner. I had a little bit of time but not much so I ate during the drive. The drive was filled with curves and straightaways that were lined with cornfields are far as the eye could see. As I made it to the residence and began my interview, a short time later I felt a slight rumble in the lower region and just sluffed it off as indigestion.

I found out the hard way that the rumbling was anything but indigestion, I was in the Defcon 1 stage and quickly on pace to reach Defcon 2 within minutes. As well as this interview was going, there was no doubt I would have to end this soon. I could feel a light sweat starting to break out and I was slowly becoming nervous due to the situation. It's not as if I hadn't experienced this feeling many times in the past because for me it was a regular occurrence, just another day at the office. Unfortunately, I didn't factor in all the variables that I would have to deal with. There was no way I could've asked to use her bathroom, it was adjoined to the living room, and exactly where the interview was taking place. If I would've relieved myself there I would've felt like she was sitting right next to me. As professional as possible, I had to end the interview and exit the house as soon as possible. Due to the fact that it was a police vehicle, I wasn't really concerned about speeding toward town realizing I still had 15 miles before any remote chance of finding an actual restroom.

I traveled about 4 miles before Defcon 3 began to create havoc in my world and I knew right then this is not going to be an ordinary relief session, I'm going to have problems just getting out of the vehicle. As I drove down a straightaway with cornfields on my left and a few houses on my right, I contemplated asking a resident to use their bathroom. The idea of approaching a house quickly faded and as Defcon 4 said "hello," I pulled the car off the side of the road next to the cornfield and put it in park as the car was still moving.

At this point, sweat and a few choice words are pouring out of me like a faucet. I knew that the cornfield was my saving grace. As I opened the car door and moved my left leg across the threshold, one unfortunate circumstance happened...Defcon 5. At this point, there was no stopping it. It was as if someone turned a faucet on inside me and I couldn't turn it off. I had to quickly disengage myself from the cloth seats and stand as quickly as possible. I ducked behind the vehicle and made my way into the first several rows of the cornfield. At this point things were not looking good. I was lying down in a cornfield and by this time I had most of my clothes off, a gun and belt lying next to me with a police radio and a cell phone.

Who do I call? I called my wife and daughter and 2 hours later they showed up with a change of clothes and an uncontrollable laugh.

EMERGENCY HEAD CALL

While in boot camp at a Marine base in North Carolina we were involved in a training exercise. The exercise involved the defending of a city. Ten Marines took part in the exercise. Eight were defenders of the city located on the perimeter in each direction, North, South, East,

West and two were attempting to infiltrate the city undetected. On this particular exercise the defenders were located in fighting holes or better known as fox holes. This was a long exercise and went well into the night. As the time progressed so too did my stomach. I knew after 6 hours there was no way I could hold it much longer.

It's tough defending a city at the Defcon 4 stage. I told my partner that I would be leaving the fighting hole and taking an emergency sitting head. The protocol for a Marine while in the field is to dig a hole with your e-tool (entrenching tool), make your deposit and cover it up when finished.

I left the fighting hole and went about 100 yards south and dug my hole. About 5 minutes later I hear the faint sound of a slight chuckle. Sure enough, as I begin my deposit, I see two Marines (infiltrators) low body crawling past me laughing as uncontrollably as possible without being detected. I couldn't alert my partner because I was too far away. Needless to say the city was overtaken by the two Marines that low body crawled past me. I had no choice. It was either dig the hole or I would have reached a Defcon 5 within a matter of minutes.

ROCKET TURD

I had a gift in high school where I could make myself fart. I would get down on all 4's and would suck air in and then force it back out. Whenever I would demonstrate this I knew I was flirting with disaster, with the poop problems I have always had. Now fast forward 6 years. I am living with the woman that would eventually become my wife, even after this incident. I was taking a shower and for some reason, I remembered how I use to make myself fart. I get out of the shower and dry off. I walk into the bedroom and my then-girlfriend was reading a book on the bed. I tell her about how I used to be able to fart continuously. I ask her if she wants to see me do it and she replied "No." I decided she needed to see it as I get down on all 4's in the bedroom, I start to suck in air, but I can't fart like I use to. I decide to let the air build-up. I feel a really good fart is about to happen so I force it out. The most awful wet-sounding fart comes out. My girlfriend asks if I shit and I reach back and don't feel anything. I tell her I don't think I did. I get up and there is nothing on the floor behind me, so I think I am in the clear. My girlfriend is walking around the room and then screams in horror. I asked her what was wrong. She tells me to look. There was a basket of folded clean laundry on the floor about 6 feet from where I was trying to fart. Nestled on top of the folded clothes was a single turd. I didn't know until that day that I could shoot a turd that far.

SHE MARRIED ME AFTER DEFCON 5

It was our first date and it started out like any other date in high school, go to the mall and then to eat. It's where the eating part really made things interesting. Our dinner consisted of nothing but trigger food for me, which is Mexican food. Before we left the restaurant I went to the restroom, TWICE. As we leave the restaurant and exit the parking lot it hits me like a ton of bricks. I sped to the closest gas station and put the truck in park. My date is probably wondering what is happening. I parked the truck in the side rear of the lot because I knew I would never make it into the store. As I exited the truck it all came out. I quickly waddled to the side of the building and leaned against it. I peeked around the corner and asked my date to throw me the knife in my glovebox. My intent was to cut off my pants and underwear. She threw the knife; she threw it 25 feet over my head. As I continued to lean against the wall, a woman passes by in disbelief at what she is seeing, a half-naked man with poop all over him. That was my first date and we are still married 20 years later.

BEAGLES AND WINGS

It was rabbit season and we were all excited, especially the beagles. As the morning progressed so did my stomach. I had to go pretty bad. I decided if I didn't go now then Defcon 5 would pay a visit that I wasn't ready for. I found the nearest large tree and leaned against it. Of course about 10 seconds later I hear the beagles being released from the boxes. As I'm making progress, so too are the beagles. In the middle of a deposit, one beagle actually ran under my legs, at the tree and took a heavy brunt of poop. His entire backside was covered. Shortly thereafter, I saw his owner dunking the beagle's body in the lake not far from where we were hunting. A lesson has been learned; do not eat spicy chicken wings the night before an early hunt.

DID YOU CHANGE YOUR CLOTHES?

During the summer I was invited to a church group outing with a friend at a local amusement park. As I stood in line for a rollercoaster, I felt the rumblings in my stomach. I quickly left the line and headed for the nearest restroom. As I made my way in, there was only one stall and two people waiting. I waited patiently until there was one left. As I stood at the sink, I asked the person in the stall if they were going to be much longer, he said "I'll be right out." No sooner than I asked, I felt the release, a release I couldn't stop when it started. As I finished with diarrhea in my pants and down my legs, the toilet flushed. I made my way into the toilet and cleaned up as much as possible. I left a trail from the sink to the stall. I left the restroom area and found a security guard who took me to the first aid office where they gave me a shower and a change of clothes. When I finally made it back to my friend he asked, "Did you change your clothes?"

SINKHOLE

One day while working, I could feel my stomach working up a good one. I didn't want to have to stop because I was in a bad area of town. I started to sweat and dance in my car and I knew I had held it too long. I pulled off at a restaurant and I ran as fast as I could to the restroom. I was saying a prayer that the stall would be open because I knew it was my only hope. I entered the restroom and saw feet in the stall. At this point, I started to accept that I was going to poop my pants. I ask the guy if he was almost finished and he said "no." I then had only one option; I dropped my pants and pooped in the sink. I turned the water on and tried to wash it down but that wasn't happening. I had to wipe with paper towels and throw them in the trashcan. I heard the guy in the stall ask what was going on out there. I just fled as fast as I could

FISH POOP

I was on a family vacation in Destin, Florida. I was about 30 yards out off-shore in the beautiful Gulf of Mexico. Suddenly I went to an immediate Defcon 3. I looked up at the beach and saw how far the bathroom was and realized there is no way I would make it. Even though the water and area was packed, I decided I had to release it into the ocean. I swam out as far away from people as I could. I went underwater and dropped my pants. I then let my bowels release. I hurried up and pulled my pants back up and swam back towards the beach with my family. I thought I had pulled it off and that maybe it sank, until 10 minutes later a guy near us yells, "Someone pooped out here." The turds had floated in and were among all the swimmers. I saw several people try to splash it away and others exited quickly.

IS ANYONE HOME? I'M USING YOUR CRAWL SPACE

I had a pressure washing business and was hired to pressure wash a house and the surrounding concrete. I was in the backyard when somehow, someway I skipped Defcons 1 and 2 and Defcon 3 hit me as if to say, "ha-ha I got you." I had no time to think about anything except, how can I go right now because Defcon 4 is knocking down the barriers. I was in the homeowner's backyard so I wasn't sure if anyone was home and the setup of the backyard was visible to the surrounding neighbors. I scrambled in desperation and saw an opening under the porch. Upon further inspection it happened to be their crawl space. Everything is fair game at this point......I'm going in. As I got on my hands and knees I made my way into the crawl space and by some miracle I was able to get in a position to relieve myself. As I'm in the space, I hear someone above the floor board say, did you hear that noise? Of course, at that point, I realized they were home and I think they were talking about me. I immediately sped up the process and was able to relieve myself, get dressed and crawl out of the space before they came into the backyard. They eventually did come to the backyard asked if I saw a rodent go in their crawlspace. I said I don't know but just in case I wouldn't go in there.

Share your journey of how you bobbed and weaved, overcame close calls, dodged that one moment of an unfortunate circumstance, or maybe how that unfortunate circumstance owned you.

Email your journey

POTTYBRAKE11@GMAIL.COM

It will be posted on the following website

WWW.POTTYBRAKE.US

Thank you to those who
contributed their thoughts and ideas

Rick Bernecker ~ Chad Dance ~ Joe Steimle

SUPPORT THOSE WHO SERVE YOU

REFERENCES

1. https://www.powerthesaurus.org/toilet/synonyms; Date 5-16-2022

2. https://www.wordhippo.com/what-is/another-word-for/doing_number_two.html; Date 05-14-2022

3. http://onlineslangdictionary.com/thesaurus/words+meaning+to+defecate,+poop,+shit.html; Date 5-16-2022

4. https://aboutibs.org/what-is-ibs/facts-about-ibs; Date 03-28-2022

5. https://www.betterhealth.vic.gov.au/health/conditionsandtreatments/shy-bladder-syndrome; Date 02-04-2023

Made in the USA
Middletown, DE
29 May 2023

31058135R00046